Me Love to SHARE with Cookie Monster

A Book about Generosity

Marie-Therese Miller

Lerner Publications ◆ Minneapolis

Sesame Street's mission has always been about teaching kids much more than simply the ABCs and 123s. This series of books about nurturing the positive character traits of generosity, respect, empathy, positive thinking, resilience, and persistence will help children grow into the best versions of themselves. So come along with your funny, furry friends from Sesame Street as they learn about making themselves—and the world—smarter, stronger, and kinder.

—Sincerely, the Editors at Sesame Street

TABLE OF CONTENTS

What Is Sharing?

Being generous means giving to others.

Me share me football.

You can be generous by sharing.

How to Share

You share your toy with a friend.

What can you share?

Your friend plays with it and then gives it back.

Sharing is one way to show people that you care about them.

9

You can share some of what you have with another person.

Me break cookie in half to share.

11

Sometimes we share by taking turns.

When did you take turns?

You can take turns on a swing. Your friend swings, and then you swing.

13

You can share work. You might help your dad stir the pancake batter.

I help Mommy wash and fold clothes.

Sharing work helps the task go faster and makes it more fun!

You can share your time with others.

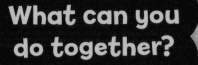

What can you do together?

You can bike with your grandma or read to your brother.

You can share your talents and your ideas.

I play my guitar and sing for my friends and family.

You might tell funny jokes or write stories.

19

Being generous feels good.

BE A BUDDY!

Make a picture with your friend. Share your crayons, paints, and ideas. How do you feel when you share?

Glossary

generous: giving to others

idea: a thought

talent: a special skill

turn: a chance to do something

work: to do a job

Learn More

Miller, Marie-Therese. *Everyone Has Value with Zoe: A Book about Respect.* Minneapolis: Lerner Publications, 2021.

Pettiford, Rebecca. *Showing Generosity.* Minneapolis: Bullfrog Books, 2017.

Shepherd, Jodie. *Kindness and Generosity: It Starts with Me!* New York: Children's Press, 2016.

Index

Photo Acknowledgments

Additional image credits: Rawpixel.com/Shutterstock.com, p. 4; Jaren Jai Wicklund/Shutterstock.com, pp. 5, 15; spass/Shutterstock.com, p. 6; Juliya Shangarey/Shutterstock.com, p. 7; fizkes/Shutterstock.com, p. 8; FamVeld/Shutterstock.com, p. 9; Monkey Business Images/Shutterstock.com, p. 10; szefei/Shutterstock.com, pp. 11, 16; Oleg Mikhaylov/Shutterstock.com, p. 12; A3pfamily/Shutterstock.com, p. 13; bbernard/Shutterstock.com, p. 14; Pavel Kobysh/Shutterstock.com, p. 17; Vasilyev Alexandr/Shutterstock.com, p. 18; LightField Studios/Shutterstock.com, p. 19; Patrick Foto/Shutterstock.com, p. 20.

For my best friend, Donna, who has shared her generous spirit and her laughter with me for sixty years

Lerner Publications Company
An imprint of Lerner Publishing Group, Inc.
241 First Avenue North
Minneapolis, MN 55401 USA

For reading levels and more information, look up this title at www.lernerbooks.com.

Main body text set in Billy Infant. Typeface provided by SparkyType.

Editor: Rebecca Higgins **Designer:** Emily Harris **Photo Editor:** Brianna Kaiser

Library of Congress Cataloging-in-Publication Data

Names: Miller, Marie-Therese, author.
Title: Me love to share with Cookie Monster : a book about generosity / Marie-Therese Miller.
Description: Minneapolis : Lerner Publications, [2021] | Series: Sesame street character guides | Includes bibliographical references and index. | Audience: Ages 4–8 | Audience: Grades K–1 | Summary: "Cookie Monster is a friend to all on Sesame Street, and kids will love learning from this funny, furry character how to share toys, help others, and be a good friend"— Provided by publisher.
Identifiers: LCCN 2020009489 (print) | LCCN 2020009490 (ebook) | ISBN 9781728403946 (library binding) | ISBN 9781728418711 (ebook)
Subjects: LCSH: Sharing—Juvenile literature. | Sesame Street (Television program)—Juvenile literature.
Classification: LCC BJ1533.G4 M55 2021 (print) | LCC BJ1533.G4 (ebook) | DDC 177/.7—dc23

LC record available at https://lccn.loc.gov/2020009489
LC ebook record available at https://lccn.loc.gov/2020009490

Manufactured in the United States of America
1-48394-48908-6/17/2020